How Animals Care for Their Babies

by Roger B. Hirschland

Ducklings follow their parents closely. Can you find all 14 babies?

BOOKS FOR YOUNG EXPLORERS
NATIONAL GEOGRAPHIC SOCIETY

Some animals, like these monkeys,
live together in large groups.
Grown-ups and older brothers
and sisters often share
the job of protecting
the babies.

Many creatures
make nests for their babies.

Maybe you have seen a robin's nest or a squirrel's nest. But there are many nests you can't see. They are hidden under the ground or inside trees. A European rabbit collects grass for her underground nest. The grass makes a soft bed for her babies.

The northern flicker, a woodpecker, makes its nest inside a tree. It uses its sharp bill to chip an entrance hole. Then it hollows out a nest.

Some animals lay eggs and care for them.

Animals may take care of their babies
even before they hatch.
An anemone fish cleans its eggs
with its mouth. A dusky salamander
protects its eggs. This salamander lives
on wet soil near streams.

A trumpeter swan sits on her eggs and
keeps them warm. She gets up to turn
them. This keeps the temperature even.

Some animal babies
are helpless—but others are not.

Newborn white-footed mice have
pink bodies with no fur. Their eyes
and ears are closed. They must depend
on their mother. She lifts the babies
gently to move them in the nest.

A mountain goat has a full coat of hair
at birth. It can see and hear. It even
follows its mother on steep slopes
just a few hours after it is born.

Most kinds of baby birds are fed by their parents. A baby flamingo stays warm under its mother's wing as it takes food from its father's bill.

Sometimes both parents find food for their babies.

Mountain bluebirds nest in old woodpecker holes or other hidden places. To feed the young, they catch insects all day long. When a parent returns to the nest, the babies open their mouths wide. The adult pokes the food down the babies' throats.

When both parents are together, you can tell them apart easily. The father's feathers are more blue.

Some animals
nurse their young.

A mother baboon nurses her baby
with milk from her body.
Have you ever seen very young
puppies or kittens or hamsters?
Like all mammals, they drink
their mothers' milk.

A female moose stands as she nurses her young.
The mother, called a cow moose, looks around for danger
while her twin babies drink. As the calves grow older, they
will eat leaves, twigs, and water plants, just as their parents do.
The moose is the largest kind of deer.

It's time for these brown bear cubs
to begin finding their own food.
They learn how by copying
their mother. They follow her
as she catches a fish and brings it
out of the river to eat.

Animals that live in groups often help each other.

A lioness licks the coat of one of her cubs. She helps it stay clean and healthy. Lions live in family groups called prides.

An adult baboon picks through the hair of a young baboon. Monkeys spend a lot of time grooming each other this way. It helps them feel close to the others in their group.

Sometimes animal parents need to move their babies.

Why do animals move their babies? A mother elk gently pushes her tired calf to cross a river. They may find food on the other side. Baby wolf spiders ride on their mother's body for safety as she hunts for insects to eat.

A lioness carries her cub to a new hiding place so enemies won't find it. She also takes it to where there is food.

Animals protect their young in different ways.

Fuzzy loon chicks can swim just hours after they hatch.
After a day, they can even dive, like their parents.
But during their first three weeks, chicks often ride
on their parents' backs. There they stay safe and warm.

A loon may flap its wings and rise up on the water
to frighten an enemy away from its babies. Loons live
on lakes, and nest along the shore. In the spring and
summer, they make loud, sad-sounding calls.

Some birds fool their enemies rather than fight them.

The killdeer lays its eggs on the open ground. Among pebbles or gravel, the speckled eggs are hard to see. What if a fox—or you—should come along?

Fluttering along the ground, the killdeer calls out and pretends its wing is broken. The fox—or you—will probably follow the bird and never see the eggs.

Chimpanzees live in groups in the rain forests, woodlands, and grasslands of Africa. Sometimes there are only females and young in a group. The young play together, but stay near their mothers.

A chimpanzee may stay with its mother for as long as seven years. At first, the baby holds on to its mother. Even when it is big enough to run around, it often rides on her back. It still sleeps with her in a nest in the trees.

Parents stay near while their babies rest.

African elephant mothers help look after each other's young.
Sleepy babies take naps, carefully watched by the adults.
In arctic waters, white whales called belugas come to the surface
to breathe. A mother supports and protects her tired baby.

A young porcupine, which has sharp quills soon after birth, leaves its mother after eight weeks. Sooner or later, all baby animals grow up and make their way into the world.

Published by
The National Geographic Society, Washington, D. C.
Gilbert M. Grosvenor, *President and Chairman of the Board*
Melvin M. Payne, *Chairman Emeritus*
Owen R. Anderson, *Executive Vice President*
Robert L. Breeden, *Senior Vice President, Publications and Educational Media*

Prepared by
The Special Publications and School Services Division
Donald J. Crump, *Director*
Philip B. Silcott, *Associate Director*
Bonnie S. Lawrence, *Assistant Director*

Staff for this book
Jane H. Buxton, *Managing Editor*
Alison Wilbur Eskildsen, *Illustrations Editor*
Cinda Rose, *Art Director*
Rebecca Lescaze, *Researcher*
Gail N. Hawkins, *Assistant Researcher*
Sharon Kocsis Berry, *Illustrations Assistant*
Carol R. Curtis, Mary Elizabeth Ellison, Rosamund Garner, Bridget A. Johnson, Artemis S. Lampathakis, Sandra F. Lotterman,
    Eliza C. Morton, Virginia A. Williams, *Staff Assistants*

Engraving, Printing, and Product Manufacture
Robert W. Messer, *Manager*
George V. White, *Assistant Manager*
David V. Showers, *Production Manager*
George J. Zeller, Jr., *Production Project Manager*

Consultants
Eirik A. T. Blom, Maryland Ornithological Society; Ronald I. Crombie, Division of Amphibians and Reptiles, Smithsonian Institution;
    Craig Phillips, Biologist; William A. Xanten, Office of Animal Programs, National Zoological Park, Smithsonian Institution, *Scientific Consultants*
Karen O. Strimple, *Educational Consultant*
Dr. Lynda Bush, *Reading Consultant*

Illustrations Credits
Jen & Des Bartlett (cover, 21, 32); George D. Lepp/BIO-TEC IMAGES (1); Jean-Paul Ferrero/AUSCAPE (2-3); G. I. Bernard/OXFORD SCIENTIFIC FILMS (4 upper left); ANIMALS ANIMALS/Oxford Scientific Films (4-5); Tom Mangelsen (5 right, 12-13 all); ANIMALS ANIMALS/Z. Leszczynski (6 upper); Alvin E. Staffan (6 lower); Jeff Foott (7, 16-17); Dwight R. Kuhn (8 left); Tom and Pat Leeson (8-9); M. P. Kahl (10-11); William Ervin (14 left); Stephen J. Krasemann/PETER ARNOLD, INC. (14-15); Leonard Lee Rue III (18); Stephen J. Krasemann/DRK PHOTO (19); Daniel and Julie Cox (20 upper, 23 lower); Jack Dermid (20 lower); Jeanne Brakefield (22-23); Tom Brakefield (24 left); Jeff Lepore (24-25); Len Rue Jr. (28-29); Fred Bruemmer (29 lower); Alan D. Carey (30-31).
Painting on pages 26-27 by Barbara Gibson.

Library of Congress CIP Data
Hirschland, Roger B.
    How animals care for their babies.

(Books for young explorers)
Bibliography: p.
Summary: Depicts different kinds of parental behavior among a variety of animals, including the trumpeter swan, mountain goat, and baboon.
    1. Parental behavior in animals—Juvenile literature. 2. Animals—Infancy—Juvenile literature. [1. Parental behavior in animals. 2. Animals—Infancy] I. Title. II. Series.
QL762.H57   1987   591.56   87-12411
ISBN 0-87044-678-9 (regular edition)
ISBN 0-87044-683-5 (library edition)

Cover: On a plain in Africa, a Cape fox pup greets one of its parents with a lick.

Below: As fun-loving as a kitten, a lion cub playfully grabs anything that twitches— in this case, its mother's tail.

MORE ABOUT

How Animals Care for Their Babies

When you consider how animals care for their young, you probably think about the kinds of animals you are most likely to see—in the wild, in a zoo, on a farm, or in your home.

Although many of the animals most familiar to children do feed and protect their young, the vast majority of species in the animal kingdom provide no such care. Most animals, including insects, amphibians, fish, and many kinds of shellfish, hatch from eggs. The offspring never see the adults that laid and fertilized the eggs. They face life on their own.

An animal that does not take care of its young is likely to lay hundreds or even thousands of eggs. Hatchlings are often larval forms that bear little resemblance to the adult.

Many children are familiar with some kinds of larval forms—the caterpillars of moths and butterflies, and the tadpoles of frogs and toads. Such young, without parental protection, face numerous dangers, largely from predators. Their survival rate is low. Yet, animals that provide no care usually produce high enough numbers to ensure the survival of at least a few of their young—and the continuation of the species.

The cecropia moth, or robin moth (pictured on the following page), is one such animal. The female, which may grow six inches long, lays eggs in rows and cements them to the surfaces of leaves. She never returns to the eggs. The caterpillars hatch in some 15 days, ready to care for themselves. They feed on leaves for a time, then spin cocoons, pass through the pupal stage, and emerge as adult robin moths.

Many of the moth's offspring will not survive. The caterpillars are preyed upon by birds, as are the pupae in their cocoons. Adult moths are often victims of predators, disease, severe weather, and impact with automobiles. But since one female may lay as many as 400 eggs, spread among numerous leaves, the chances are good that some of the offspring will survive until they themselves can reproduce.

Among the animals that do provide care, it is usually the mother, but sometimes the mother and father together, that nurture the offspring. A notable exception is the sea horse. Like the baby short-snouted sea horses in the photograph on this page, all young sea horses emerge live from the brood pouch of an adult *male*. At mating time, female sea horses deposit as many as 200 eggs in the brood pouch below the abdomen of the male. There, the eggs are fertilized. The male holds them in his pouch for about four weeks. As the young hatch, the male expels them into the water, and they are able to swim right away.

The capabilities animals possess immediately following birth or hatching vary considerably from species to species. The young of some animals, such as mice (8),* are totally dependent on their parents for food and for protection. Other kinds of young, such as fulvous tree ducklings (1) and mountain goat kids (9), require the protection and training of their parents, but are able shortly after birth to follow the adults and eat food on their own. And finally, some animals, such as the moth caterpillar, are completely independent of their parents.

RUDIE H. KUITER

Tiny sea horses emerge from the pouch on their father's belly. The female laid eggs in the male's pouch, and he incubated them.

Even within the same class of animals, the capabilities of the newborn may vary. Altricial birds are those which hatch featherless and sightless, and depend entirely on their parents' care. Familiar altricial birds include robins, blue jays, bluebirds (12–13), and many other songbirds. In contrast, the young of such birds as the trumpeter swan (7), the loon (22–23), many ducks, geese, and other fowl, including chickens, are precocial. They follow their parents

*Numbers in parentheses refer to pages in *How Animals Care for Their Babies*.

and can find their own food immediately after hatching.

Young readers might wonder why the baby macaque (2–3) looks so different from the adults. Among several kinds of monkeys, including macaques, the young are born darker or lighter haired than their parents. Only after several months do they grow the coats characteristic of the adults.

The killdeer (24–25) is a bird youngsters might find particularly interesting to observe because of its distraction display. It feigns a broken wing to lure enemies away from its eggs. Interestingly, the killdeer displays this behavior only for predators, such as foxes, dogs, and people, that are likely to follow the bird. If a cow or a horse should approach, the killdeer—instead of pretending it is injured—will repeatedly fly at the face of the intruder until the animal leaves. Look for this bird in open fields and along shores in the United States and in much of Canada.

Children can get the best sense of how animals care for their young by observing them firsthand. Watching animals can be rewarding for you and your child in any of these places: in the home, on farms, in zoos, and in the wild.

• IN THE HOME: Observing pets at home is an excellent way for children to learn how animals care for their babies. Children should be taught, however, that all animals and their young need quiet and privacy. Too much noise or interference around animal parents may cause them to injure or abandon their own young.

• ON FARMS: If you live near a rural area, you might be able to take your child to a farm. Small family farms often raise a variety of animals. Call or write the nearest 4–H Club to find out how you can arrange a visit.

• IN ZOOS: Zoo staffs will be able to tell you which animals have had babies recently, and which exhibits to visit to find them. Look for signs at the exhibits. Some zoos have nurseries where animal babies are given special care.

• IN THE WILD: Observing animals and their young in the wild requires planning, caution, and luck. You should visit parks or wildlands in seasons when the animals are likely to have their young with them. Always be careful not to approach wildlife too closely. Adult animals often fiercely protect their young. It's a good idea to keep your distance from all wild animals. For example, you should *never* approach a moose calf (14–15) or a bear cub (16–17). The mother is likely to be nearby and may attack in defense of her young.

Birds, perhaps, are the easiest animals to observe in the wild. They may live in your area and may nest near your home. You can even encourage them to do so by setting up birdhouses or by putting out food that attracts them. You might visit parks with ponds where ducks and geese raise their young. Consult the nearest chapter of the Audubon Society or your state ornithological society or local bird club for information about the birds in your area.

ADDITIONAL READING

Amiable Little Beasts, by Roger A. Caras and Steve Graham. (New York, MacMillan Publishing Co., Inc., 1980). Family reading.

Baby Birds and How They Grow, by Jane R. McCauley. (Washington, D. C., National Geographic Society, 1983). Ages 4–8.

Book of Mammals, 2 vols. (Washington, D. C., National Geographic Society, 1981). Ages 8 and up.

The Love of Baby Animals, by Robert Burton. (New York, Crescent Books, 1976). Family reference.

Young Animals: the search for independent life, by Bernard Stonehouse. (New York, Viking Press, 1974). Family reference.

Cementing her eggs onto a leaf is the only thing a female cecropia moth will do for her young. The female now flies away and will not return. In about 15 days, larvae, or caterpillars, will hatch and take care of themselves.

DWIGHT R. KUHN